381 Days to Go. Russia-Ukraine War. Draw The Line Today.

David Gomadza

The First Global President of The World

Tomorrow's World Order

16 July 2023

ISBN: 9798852678638

DEDICATION

To Peace.
A New Better Global System of Governance, Planning and
Management.

Tomorrow's World Order

381 more days to go before the Russia-Ukraine war comes to an end.
We have decoded the brain and know everyone's thoughts. Is there a war-script everyone is following event by event date by date?
The truth will shock the hell out of you.
A MUST READ.
Visit also www.twofuture.world

Table of Contents

ACKNOWLEDGMENTS

Tomorrow's World Order

PART ONE

We as Tomorrow's World Order cannot allow this Russia /Ukraine war to continue. I as the First Global President of The World has concluded that we must intervene to stop this war. We have looked at several factors for the past five hundred days and the recent developments have made us conclude that we must do more to stop this war.

We are the new global leaders and managers and our responsibilities among others are.

1. To safeguard the existence of humanity by eliminating risks caused by the development and possible use of nuclear weapons, wars, etc.

2. To protect the lives of everyone on earth, women, children, and even your soldiers.

3. Eliminate situations that can trigger a nuclear war or a Third World War.

4. To maintain peace.

5. To protect women and children.

6. To represent those who might not be in a position to represent

themselves.

7. To advise those who might not have the correct information in terms of making informed decisions.

8. To bring perpetrators of evil acts and violence against women and children that result in deaths mainly due to wars.

9. To judge situations and conduct justice as a solution where countries, institutions, etc. are corrupt, deceptive, and use sophisticated technology to hide and deceive others.

10. To stand for justice and peace for all regardless of race, religion, ethnicity, gender, economic or social status.

First, we can proudly inform you all that we have decoded the brain. That means we know all secrets and reasons why people act the way they do. We are fair and look at the evidence we have which we publish freely in our books for all to see.

So be assured that the information we rely on is as accurate as can be. Visit our website for proof of this.

www.twofuture.world

We can easily decode the brain.

1. This means we know exactly what was said at any particular place and time.

2. We know what a person is thinking at any particular point in time.

3. We know what a person is likely to do in the future.

4. We know the future even though this is still a new area that

needs more refining.

5. We can recreate events just by looking at a person's picture.

6. We can talk to the dead and ask them who killed them, who was there when they died, and where they were at that time.

7. We can communicate with ghosts and even evil spirits.

That means we will do whatever it takes to get the truth.

Since the beginning of the war, we have given our recommendations regarding this Russia/Ukraine war. But all recommendations were specific to the period in time of the war. So, after some time the recommendations might not be appropriate to the situation at hand. But we will keep updating our recommendations as the situation changes.

You must understand that our recommendations are given in line with what we stand for and please refer to the ten reasons given at the beginning above. All our recommendations are given in line with these values and our responsibilities. That means even though your leaders might give grounds which are good to them to continue the war; even risking a nuclear weapon war. We cannot tolerate that because your leaders have only their interests at heart whereas we stand for the entire world.

The West and even Ukraine might want to continue the war until July 31, 2024, and actually give reasons they believe are right for them. To us, we stand against this because we cannot tolerate the risks of a possible nuclear war that will destroy the entire world.

Secondly, any death of a child or a woman is an attack on all of us. To some extent, even the death of your soldiers needlessly is an attack on all of us.

Mind you we are the defenders of the defenseless. Even the lives of your soldiers are protected by our laws. No leader can cause the deaths of soldiers for him or herself and his country above 50 000 without facing justice.

PART TWO

Our recommendations are specific for certain periods and conditions during the war. Recommendations given in June would apply to conditions around June mainly at the time of writing and we will update recommendations as time goes on. But the overall recommendations are in line with our responsibilities given above at the beginning.

Criteria we used for our recommendations.

We aim to eliminate the risks of having a nuclear war as the main responsibility. We also aim to save the lives of women and children who are killed by wars. Even the lives of your soldiers. We believe that where the number of deaths of soldiers exceeds 50 000, this makes us act to reduce further deaths.

Our Discovery.

The Russia/ Ukraine war is so complicated because there are so many 'invisible' players involved. It is not just a matter between Russia and Ukraine. There are other players with vested interests enough to encourage the war instead of pushing for peace. But we are not saying that this is right or wrong. Just our analysis of the reason why the war is still going on when we are there to stop wars like this one.

Our Prediction.

At the beginning, on 16 October 2022, we gave our Russia-Ukraine war Prediction based on our analysis of the situation.

https://play.google.com/store/books/details/David_Gomadza_A_Perfect_Prediction_Russia_Ukraine?id=PmaVEAAAQBAJ&hl=en_GB&gl=US

So far, our prediction is spot on. We believe that since everything we predicted has happened event by event and date by date, we are now sure that this war, if we do not intervene to stop it, will last another 381 days from today 16 July 2023. That means the war will end on 31 July 2024.

I remind you all that we have decoded the brain and can read everyone's brain thoughts. No one can lie to us.

Our Stance.

We believe that the fact that what we predicted has happened as we have predicted since 16 October 2022, we now have stronger grounds and voice to denounce the war and do whatever it takes to end this war even if this means changing all the leaders involved. Mind you we have responsibilities to safeguard the existence of all humanity by eliminating risks of a nuclear war. We safeguard the lives of women, children, and soldiers. After taking a backstage role, now, it is time, we take center stage and end this war. We have given everyone concerned the chance to act and end this war. But as you all can see, everyone involved has their own agendas and most of these will only lead to or increase the risks of a nuclear war.

As such we cannot tolerate this. We cannot let these people make decisions anymore. We are taking over the overall last-decision-making-role. I will give our reasons below.

Things have gone out of control and the risks keep increasing every day we do not act. We have analyzed the situation and sadly we cannot tolerate what is happening. We must put things in place from now on to end this war. Even if the war continues now there will be judgment in the end for all concerned.

PART THREE

The conditions that have triggered the need for us to act with immediate effect.

1. Ukraine's resilience and fighting.

No one would have expected Ukraine to be still standing against the Russians. At the beginning of the war, few believed Ukraine would be still standing five hundred days after the invasion. Ukraine has become the defender of NATO, not the other way round. I would not be surprised if NATO refused Ukraine's NATO membership application. Surely if Ukraine can fight Russia this way, why would they need NATO's membership? Surely Ukraine can stand for itself. I think no one in NATO expected this resilience. NATO now can think twice about Ukraine's membership. Surely Ukraine can stand for itself. NATO can consider or advocate for a secret alliance with Ukraine instead of taking Ukraine as a member. Ukraine can fight for itself even if it means sacrificing its people. NATO is the one that needs Ukraine and because of this will form a secret alliance. This will be to make Russia pay for the deaths of the people and the destruction of the infrastructure as Russia will refuse to pay citing Ukraine's request for the most destructive weapons as contributory to their mishaps.

To us, this is a substantial risk.

a} Yes Ukraine has proved that it does not even need NATO to defeat Russia. Five hundred days is a long time and we even predicted that they would withstand Russia's attacks even furthermore: making the war end in July 2024. Meaning another 381 days of fighting without succumbing to Russia. This can make Russia think of using nuclear weapons citing the West's own acts against Japan as precedence. Surely for a country like Russia to be defeated by a small country like Ukraine is not just humiliating but can pose an existential threat to Russia. This is because NATO will now want to flex their muscle as well; only because they will have witnessed Russia be defeated by Ukraine. Witnessing Russia's struggle to win against Ukraine will give them wings to want to do even better than Ukraine.

The danger here is that Russia will now think seriously about the use of nuclear weapons.

b} Russia now can suspect or be afraid of a secret alliance between Ukraine and NATO, that instead of withdrawing their troops they will fully invade Ukraine. This is to effect regime change because now they will not trust Ukraine because of the secret alliance. The risks are that NATO now in a secret alliance treaty with Ukraine will in the future have to come to the rescue. This will mean a war worse than a nuclear war.

c}Russia can take advantage of the situation and consider Ukraine as equally strong as them. Probably strong enough to defeat them that they might consider the use of nuclear weapons on them. Ukrainians' stubbornness and resilience can weaken NATO that in the future might not help as they now believe that Ukrainian can defend themselves.

d} Other risks will come from Ukraine itself. After defending itself from Russia and after the West's rejection of its NATO membership only on grounds that it does not need NATO's protection. Will make the West form a secret alliance that will mean the supply of nuclear weapons to Ukraine to match the threat at hand. Yes, instead of Russia being the one threatening to use nuclear weapons. Now it will be Ukraine threatening if not using these in Russia. We believe the Russians have noticed this and the Wagner revolt is a smokescreen to cover their second plan. That of the Wagner to be ready to deploy nuclear weapons from Belarus as they might have suspected a secret alliance between Ukraine and NATO. One that will make NATO supply nuclear weapons to Ukraine. You must understand this is different from what I argued below. I argued that Ukraine can publicly request a nuclear weapon as a deterrent and for self-defense. This is different from nuclear weapons issued under a secret alliance. This is because the public request is meant to deter Russia from threatening and attacking. All this to bring them to the negotiating table. The dangers of a secret alliance's nuclear weapon issue are that this can be deployed. Its purpose is not to deter but to destroy. It does not matter if it is for self-defense or not.

e} The fact that Russia has thousands of nuclear weapons and knows the risks involved. They might be aggravated and attack to effect regime change before things go wrong.

f} The West's public utterances to offer cluster bombs to Ukraine can aggravate Russia. This is because Ukraine is going to use cluster bombs in occupied annexed areas to push away those loyal to Russians. It is like the use of landmines. That if we cannot get the land. Then no one can live on that land. This means the cluster bombs just like the landmines are to push away those loyal to the Russians. This means Russia will have lost the war. This could be what the West is referring to by saying that Russia has lost the war already. The Russians. To protect those loyal to the Russians they might aggressively attack to effect regime change. To prevent the extensive use of these cluster bombs.

2. The increased risks of World War Three.

Surely, we could have had a Third World War by the 11 of July 2023 if NATO had accepted Ukrainian's membership. This is how bad and critical the situation has become. If NATO had accepted Ukrainian membership on the 11 of July 2023 that would have meant NATO defending Ukraine with Russia still in Ukraine that would have meant a big war. We also believe that Russia's allies would have joined in. A Third World War.

3. A potential secret acceptance of Ukrainian membership to ambush Russia.

The West as per our prediction of 16 October 2022 can easily secretly accept Ukrainian membership and call all reservists preparing for a war with Russia. Especially now that Sweden has already joined NATO. That brings me to the next point. A major risk

4. The Risks of a Nuclear War have increased significantly.

I explained above that we predicted a working hypothesis. That prediction has come true, and this has changed the situation. The once-perceived risks have now become real. The risks of a nuclear weapons war have increased significantly.

The huge losses of Russian soldiers will only trigger the need to act eventually.

The fact that the West as of 16 July 2023 is now convinced that Russia has lost the war will only trigger the need to match the threat at hand. This means that Russia will start feeling inferior to Ukraine and the West. We all know that the only way to match the threat at hand is to resort to powerful weapons and barbaric methods. This means an option to use nuclear weapons. The West used this option in the Japanese War.

5. The West's admittance to the supply and use of cluster bombs.

This is in two parts. First as an increased risk to the deaths of women and children. Cluster bombs are known to increase civilian casualties. Ukraine is believed to have acknowledged the receipt of these cluster bombs from the West. Secondly, the use of these dangerous weapons on civilians might give Russia precedence in using even deadly weapons like nuclear weapons. If Ukraine can risk its people to win the war. Russia might risk a Third World War to win this war.

6. Huge loss of Russian soldiers estimated on 16 July 2023 as 47 000 by independent media.

https://apnews.com/article/russia-ukraine-war-military-deaths-facd75c2311ed7be660342698cf6a409

 Any huge loss of soldiers poses an existential threat especially if Russia is to properly defend itself against a possible NATO invasion. This can only mean the use of nuclear weapons in the future to match the threat at hand in Ukraine and its allies in NATO and the West.

7. The Wagner revolt.

In our Russia-Ukraine war prediction, we predicted a revolt in Russia but in August 2023 even though this will be defeated and controlled.

Our concern is to do with this as a need for a new strategy due to the huge losses of the Russian soldiers. The revolt highlights the frustration of those on the battleground and the need to act to rectify the situation. This could be in two ways.

First is the need for new strategies. We predicted that between July and September Belarus would enter the war and attack Kyiv from Belarus. This Wagner revolt can be an arrangement to fulfill our prediction. It is not Belarus that will attack Kiv from the top but the Wagner group that will invade from Belarus. Secondly, our concern is with the fact that the Wagner invasion will make the Kremlin leadership consider minimizing the loss of Russian soldiers by the use of lethal weapons. If the West can use these to save their soldiers' lives. What stops them from defending themselves from an existential threat in the West and NATO? Thirdly this is a wake-up call for the Kremlin leadership itself. Now they know if they do not act to defend their soldiers some of the soldiers might revolt. Mind you this is not the end of the revolution as we predicted another revolution is due in August. Unless if they are bringing everything forward by one month.?

8. NATO's decision on Ukraine's enrollment on 11 July 2023.

NATO's indecisiveness can prolong the war. I know that NATO put a condition for Ukraine's enrollment; that is; that, it must not be at war with Russia. This without reading between the lines might mean Ukraine acting now to end the war. But knowing what the Ukrainian situation is can highlight that the intended reason is to prolong the war. Now Ukraine cannot go back. Are in a catch-22. Five hundred days and everything has already been destroyed with more than 20 000 soldiers dead. Now more than ever before; they need the West's assistance in rebuilding Ukraine after refusing all avenues for peace offered by Russia. After insisting on the need to fight. Now they have no other options left than to fight until 31 July 2024.

Russia on the other hand knowing that NATO will not intervene will continue the war. This is because surrendering without regime change in Ukraine is a failure. Giving up will only invite NATO to consider invading. All this means the war will end in July 2024. Imagine what can go wrong between now and July 2024. Imagine the number of innocent women and children who will have died needlessly. Imagine the soldiers who will have died then. Ukraine relied heavily on NATO's specific decision on when they will join the alliance. This July could be the time they expected the war to end. Another year to go. Hence the title of this book. Another 381 days to go is too long and both Russia and Ukraine might not have the power and will to continue to fight. I know all this could be good for NATO if they are considering invading or weakening Russia in the future.

But from our point of view, this increases the risks of a nuclear war. The more the war goes on. Surely the more Russia is weakened. To such a point that they will consider the use of nuclear weapons. In order to defend against an existential threat.

We cannot leave things to chance. We have precedence in the Japanese situation. Then it was not as horrific as it can be this time because Russia itself has the most nuclear weapons whereas Japan did not have any.

If you can promise us that if one uses nuclear weapons, then the other is not able to use theirs then we might say we have nothing to worry about that much. But this is not the case.

9. Reverting to the past for answers. Presence of a war-script.

I explained in my book Tomorrow's World Order
https://play.google.com/store/books/details/David_Gomadza_Tom
orrow_s_World_Order?id=VDauDwAAQBAJ

That the stage of development humanity is in is a defensive one. One where humanity makes weapons and uses the weapons to drive the economy. So, wherever there is economic stagnation and high inflation. Humanity will trigger wars. To correct the imbalance caused by investing huge resources in defense and weapon manufacturing. All this at the expense of other areas. Like technological development. The system will become stagnant as resources are used to make weapons when all countries are becoming friends, meaning no wars. Your leaders over the years have gone back to the past to look for solutions. That meant going back to the 1660s picking up a script of events then. Then using that same script. Exactly event by event to trigger wars. All this to be able to easily predict what is going to happen next. They can manipulate how events develop. The danger here is that it becomes impossible to intervene to stop the war.

This is the problem with the current war. They are following an already written war-script. Fact.

We gave our recommendations before we discovered that there is a war-script that everyone is following. This is the script that we have used to predict that the war will end in July 2024.

This explains why our recommendations did not work. As you will find out, it is because there are a lot of players involved all with their own agendas.

But all I can say right now is that all these people; they have no regard for a nuclear war or the deaths of women and children. Hence our rise to power. Humanity is born to square up and muscle each other and to show who is boss. In the past, yes, this was tolerated because of the lack of nuclear weapons but now things have changed. No one wins a nuclear war.

10. Possibility of a Culling strategy or the need to disperse people to fulfill labor shortages in other areas.

Our responsibility is to protect the lives of women and children who have no one to defend them. Sanctions, economic and financial problems, technological advancement, etc., and simply evil. All this has meant some people breaking all the rules. All this to cull people for whatever reason they consider just. Or the need to drive out people from a country to fulfill labor shortages somewhere else; all can be the reasons behind some tactics.

11. A business model where one country benefits financially from all this war.

Extortion and a business model where one country enslave another country digitally and invisible to the naked eye. Then triggers a war using a script from the past. Then force the nation to siphon money and send it to this country. Only after burdening the country with loans that must be repaid. The model works like this.

A country uses a script from the 1660s event by event. Over the years, they plan everything, triggering conditions to get the country into a war. When the country wants peace, they encourage the country to fight, telling them that they will win. That country fights hard hoping for a way out that they might have been promised. For example, given a date to join NATO. So, they fight hard for the date. The whole country's infrastructure is destroyed. Any money requested from other countries used to build back some of the infrastructure is wasted as the new infrastructure is destroyed. Until the country realizes that it is better to pay up the extorting country. This is because the extorting country will be telling it that it is helping it to get money from other countries and must pay it first by siphoning money to this country. But the country will refuse, resulting in continued destruction of the new infrastructure repaired or built. There will come a point when the country siphons the money out. The extorting country will start talking about huge corruption to give the leader an alibi because he or she will need to account for the money. When an opportunity to stop the war arises e.g., NATO simply gives a date when for example Ukraine will join up. They will now even consider refusing it altogether. The country is rendered unable to defend itself in the very sense of the phrase that it is left dependent on the extorting country. A country in huge debt loses sovereignty and becomes a hostage. The whole idea of this is to cull all 'deadwood' for the country to be able to pay back the loans. Most of these loans were forced on it and all taken back or destroyed in that any infrastructure built by the loans is subsequently destroyed. Leaving the country without anything to show for that loan.

Again, you must understand that we stand to defend those rendered incapable of defending themselves unfairly.

12. The inability for anyone to stop the war or to put things in place to work towards stopping the war.

I can say that there is no one out there who can stop this war. As I explained above there are a lot of people with vested interests. All with the long-term goal of prolonging the war to July 2024. We believe that the war has reached intolerable levels from every angle you want to look at it. The number of civilian casualties has reached intolerable figures. The huge deaths of soldiers from both sides, now reaching 50 000, cannot be tolerated. The huge destruction of infrastructure, especially civilian ones, has made this a humanitarian crisis. The position in which Ukraine is in. In limbo now, where it cannot stop the war. This, after refusing all avenues of peace. Only after being encouraged to fight and the failure of NATO to give them guarantees in terms of dates. Even though

NATO included a condition for enrolment. This is empty because if NATO wanted the war to end. They would simply have given a date of joining at least a month or two away to allow Russia to remove their troops from Ukraine. Encouraging them to fight can only prolong the war.

Do not get us wrong, we are not against the West, NATO, or even Russia. We stand for everyone. As a manager of the world to safeguard the existence of all humanity, this is our fair analysis of the situation without vested interests apart from what our responsibilities are.

PART FOUR

How do we stop this war?

We cannot let the war go on until July 2024.

Russia's Situation.

Russia will or has lost grounds for justifying invading Ukraine as the war continues over five hundred days now. This is because the number of soldiers who have died would have been many and high enough to justify withdrawal. Mind you Russia had predicted Kyiv would fall within days. As time goes by NATO who might have feared Russia in the first place now after witnessing Ukrainians defeat them. Will want to keep their reputation as defenders of small nations and attack Russia. This is because if Ukraine itself can defeat Russia, then why would Ukraine need the protection of NATO? NATO can be justified to refuse Ukraine's membership on the grounds that NATO would need Ukraine's assistance as they would have defeated the mighty Russians.

Ukrainian's situation.

1. We believe NATO is like a cult and uses gangster tactics [no offense]. To join the cult, one must prove worthiness. That means to fight to death a country to which you are close. In order to gain their trust as a counter to a Trojan horse argument. The conditions

are according to its demands no matter what. If they say Ukraine must fight until July 2024 that is what is to happen no matter what.

2. NATO itself has its requirements like the number of dependencies, the economic stamina of Ukraine, and their ability to service their loans without putting a burden on NATO members. This can mean the need to reduce dependents. Meaning they might keep conditions to fight on.

3. Ukraine might believe for sure that victory and peace can only come by defeating Russia on the battlefield and rightly so. But their need to join NATO pose an existential threat to Russia. This means that they might want to press hard to put NATO off being a future problem. We are not against countries that fight for their sovereignty. In fact, sovereignty is one of our core principles as Tomorrow's World Order. **To us, the death of a woman or child or your soldiers over fifty thousand is an attack on all of us.** Where the possibilities are against the odds or where a lot of people have to die first when other options are available, we cannot tolerate this. To us we must ask one question; Does Ukraine know that this war will end in July 2024? If so, are they prepared to fight another 381 days? Above all at what cost?

If they know and are prepared to fight another 381 days, then it is up to them. As I explained in other books, see appendix; we can apportion the deaths of civilians or even soldiers to the leadership if they knew all conditions but still continued with the war. Where other options are available.

Does Ukraine know that stubbornness; one that results in needless deaths of civilians. And opting for the same conditions, as now in the end, after huge civilian deaths. Can be regarded as intolerable criminal acts? I argued that fighting without a strong strategy can only improve the bargaining position of Ukraine and has nothing to do with peace or freedom. I highlighted in the last recommendations that if Ukraine were serious about ending the war, they would arm themselves with nuclear weapons to match the threat in Russia.

It is an option open to them. If the West can find it justified to provide cluster bombs that are known to kill civilians surely it can be justified to arm them with nukes as well as a deterrent. If one nation can tell the world that they have sent their nuke to Ukraine for them to use it as a defense and deterrence, surely Russia will reconsider its position. If NATO is to give a date of Ukraine's joining its alliance. Surely that will make Russia think again.

I am not saying that Ukraine must be given nuclear weapons to use. We are against the use of nuclear weapons but if that brings Russia to the negotiating table it is better this way than for an all-out nuclear war.

Fear sometimes is the means to everyone's downfall. I believe in fighting fire with fire as a deterrent that works. What you can do to others can be done to you too.

What can Ukraine do?

1. The Ukrainians, were right to demand to be told the date of joining NATO.

2. Must assess if they have the means and will to fight until July 2024.

3. Must calculate the cost in terms of human lives and further destruction of the infrastructure.

4. They can still negotiate peace with Russia.

5. If they still want to fight, they can do so but must know all

outcomes.

6. They can request weapons from the West and NATO but must aim to get all the weapons they need now to use until July 2024. I argued in the last recommendations that if we are correct. The West will use the rationing-of-weapons tactic to prolong the war. Giving certain weapons when they see it fit and all this not for the Ukrainians to win but to prolong the war.

7. Request loans to be written off now rather than later.

Russia's Situation

Russia can simply recalculate its stance and reconsider the whole thing. They can easily end this war by pulling their troops from Ukraine.

1. Russia must check if they are prepared to fight for another 381 days.

2. Must check if they can sacrifice any more soldiers and resources until July 2024.

3. Russia must realize that sanctions are meant to make them prolong the war and cull their troops. The temptation to do so is high. Too much pressure can result in neglect. Which can cause revolt. One of the goals of enforcing sanctions.

4. Russia should consider the possibility of NATO secretly accepting Ukraine's membership to ambush them. They must now seriously consider the possibility of NATO grouping calling reservists behind the scenes in preparation for war. They must ask if they are prepared to defend their country if NATO attacks.

5. Russia must acknowledge that a 500-day-old war means a tough

war for an expected four-day war. In that case, they must reconsider the invasion.

6. They can now opt for peace to avoid a war with NATO. They must assume as if NATO has already accepted Ukrainian membership. As I said, NATO can secretly accept Ukrainian membership applications. Or enter into a secret alliance to supply deadly weapons like nukes.

7. Given the demanding situation and the West's support of Ukraine, Russia can simply count their losses and withdraw its troops.

8. Russia must ask itself what it would have done if NATO had accepted Ukrainian's membership on the 11 of July.

9. Russia must ask itself if it is prepared to fight NATO and start a Third World War. Surely, we could have had a Third World War by 11 July. This is how terrible things have gone. Surely a situation we cannot tolerate.

10. The big question to ask is this? Has NATO secretly accepted Ukrainian membership or even worse formed a secret partnership alliance with Ukraine|? Where they supply them with nuclear weapons to defend themselves? Is a Third World War still a possibility?

11. Would Russia allow the use of cluster bombs in their annexed regions? Especially knowing that cluster bombs will act like landmines? Rendering the land useless for inhibition by anyone. Russia can use this fact to aggressively invade and attack Ukraine to effect Regime change and prevent use of these dangerous bombs.

12. Russia can be forced to use nuclear weapons on Ukraine as a

way of making the United States be held accountable for their dropping of nuclear bombs on Japan. Russia can justify the use of nuclear weapons as a way of highlighting making the USA be held accountable as it can argue that they walked away. If it has to face justice, it must do so only after the USA has been held accountable for its atrocities in the Japan saga. This can lead to a nuclear war and a Third World War.

NATO and the West's situation.

NATO now can look at Ukraine differently after its show of good-stubbornness and resilience. Surely if we want to be truthful NATO needs Ukraine to fight their dirty war as a proxy. Ukraine stood its ground and five hundred days after the invasion they are still standing. We believe they can stand another 381 days to July 2024. I would not be surprised if NATO refused their membership. This is because NATO protects weak members. If Ukraine can defeat Russia, then why do they need NATO? We believe that this fact among other reasons might make NATO reject Ukraine's membership and instead offer them a secret alliance. An alliance to come to their rescue and provide weapons when needed. Above all to provide secret nuclear weapons to use as a deterrent or to defend themselves.

NATO might have good intentions to help Ukraine. But we believe if they wanted to stop this war, they would have simply accepted Ukraine's membership as a deterrent. Announcing a joining date would have indirectly ordered Russia out of Ukraine. But might have aggravated the situation into a Third World War.

PART FIVE

Our Situation as Tomorrow's World Order.

To us, as Tomorrow's World Order, we believe that it is better to have a fair Third World War than have a secret alliance that will lead to a nuclear war. Boys will always be boys, especially regarding muscling out each other. Boys what to play with their toys. This is within their DNA. A Third World War will mean the easiest system change for us. After all these warmongers kill each other. I will put my new system as Tomorrow's World Order with ease. In fact, without shading any blood, keeping my hands clean. So, we should let you kill each other but fairly without the use of nuclear weapons. No one will win a nuclear war.

The reason behind our stance is that the problem is the current system that relies on wars as a means of introducing relief to the system. Without wars, the system will collapse but not completely to effect a system change. This is because the West put things in place to avoid a complete system collapse in NATO, the World Bank, and the IMF. These institutions are like wires placed in place of a fuse. I explained in Tomorrow's World Order that every system has fuses that can explode and burn so that a system overload will result in a collapse. When this happens, this means the need for a better new system. But after the Second World War, the West mainly established NATO, the IMF, and the World Bank to replace the fuse in order to prevent a complete collapse. But having the same system. Over the years this has worked. This is because the IMF and World Bank are used to provide loans to poor countries or other countries like Ukraine. The conditions of the loans like the Economic Structural Adjustment Program mean the culling of all dependents, even the soldiers of the borrowing country.

Culling: The Sad Reality of The IMF and World Bank Loans as Triggers of Wars.: Finding Solutions to The Russian-Ukraine War.

https://play.google.com/store/books/details/David_Gomadza_Culling_The_Sad_Reality_of_The_IMF_a?id=mMluEAAAQBAJ

In reality, there are no other means to reduce these dependents, apart from pandemics and wars. NATO alliance prevents any other countries from protesting as the West puts sanctions and conditions to trigger a war. Even the East like Russia adopts the same tactics. NATO in turn will offload the huge weapons stockpiles to support the invaded country. This restarts the cycle. The reason for the stagnant economy and high inflation would have been the huge stockpiles of weapons. Wars create pressure valves that release and relieve the pressure in the system. That means new weapons supply demands. And more manufacturing of weapons. Lastly and a new demand for funding defense.

So, the only solution is to change this defensive stage we are in with a system that is powered by technology instead of weapons manufacturing. If there is no demand for weapons. That means the current system will only function properly for twenty years after which a war is needed to relieve the pressure and restart the cycle again. Meaning forever wars. Hence the need for a new system that relies on technological advancement as a driver of the economy and not wars as in weapons manufacturing.

Risks of a nuclear war.

We aim to remove all the risks of a nuclear war even if that means arming Ukraine with a nuclear weapon. This is because sometimes to end a nuclear war is to arm both parties with nuclear weapons as a way of matching the threat and magnitude of threat at hand.

But overall, we aim to maintain peace.

Defending the defenseless.

Only we can stand for the rights of women and children who die needlessly because of wars. Our protection extends to your soldiers as well. We are against the sacrificing of soldiers cheaply. That means some factors cannot be tolerated no matter what. The sacrifice of soldiers above 50 000 cannot be accepted. No leader, soldier or country will sacrifice a large number of their soldiers where there is no existential direct threat. Russia must prove that failure to win the war, meaning regime change in Kyiv, will pose an existential threat to justify the deaths of soldiers above 50,000. We must intervene and assess the situation from an independent global leader's point of view. We must advise on possible avenues of peace. Your soldiers' lives are protected by our laws. We are saying this because we believe that if we do not intervene there are 381 more days to fight this war until July 2024.

Russia and even Ukraine must ask themselves how many soldiers they will have lost until July 2024. They must assess if there are other ways to reduce the number of deaths of their soldiers. They must assess and evaluate peace negotiations. They must assess the level of difficulty in achieving their goals, especially considering that they thought that Kyiv will fall in days and considering that they will fight for more than 881 days in total. Meaning 381 days to go. The use of cluster bombs by both the Russians and the

Ukrainians can pose huge risks to civilians.

The death of a child or woman is an attack on all of us.

We must do whatever it takes to protect the lives of women and children.

There are a lot of issues to be addressed regarding everyone, Russia, Ukraine, The West, NATO, and other players.

PART SIX

OUR RECOMMENDATIONS AND DEMANDS AS TOMORROW'S WORLD ORDER.

1.

Russia.

a} Must pull out their soldiers from a sovereign country. We stand against the invasion of sovereign states. Few grounds can be used to justify invading a sovereign country and we believe this case is not strong enough to justify these grounds. The reason is that Russians and Ukrainians can be regarded as related in every sense of the word. The language, same backgrounds as part of the Soviet Union, similarities, marriages, etc. make the justification for the cruel treatment of one group weak. We as Tomorrow's World Order can order a country to attack another where it can be proved that the grounds for cruel treatment of diverse groups exist. The case is justified whether the people concerned are different or not. Different people by nature can be cruel to each other because they are different. This is a convincing case for such an invasion, but we do not believe that this ground is justified.

But the use of cluster bombs can justify such invasion as these cluster bombs can kill civilians and render the land useless. But only if Russia itself did not use cluster bombs. If it has used the cluster bombs itself first, then this ground cannot be relied upon.

b} Even if they had initial grounds the period that has passed can put Russia in the footstep of Ukraine making them do more to their people in soldiers what they are complaining about in Ukraine. A long war can strain the soldiers to breaking points without rotation. Insufficient supplies etc. will put the soldiers in the steps of the people they are trying to liberate thereby making Russia itself guilty of the same crimes they have highlighted. We believe that if Russia wanted regime change they could have gone straight to Kyiv through Belarus.

After five hundred days of fighting without critical changes to the tactics, we can start questioning Russia's real motive in invading Ukraine. This is in light of the sanctions imposed by the West. Sanctions are meant to punish and put a government in a corner to make them unable to support even their soldiers. So sanctioned governments would embark on wars first to address the issues. But over time the war fields became grinding machines. The more soldiers die the relief to the system as long as the sanctions are in place or keep being added or increased. In the end, the government is reluctant to act fast to correct the situation. The other party can intensify the sanctions now to trigger a revolt because by now the other soldiers will notice the lack of care in the lives of the soldiers that are dying. The Wagner Revolution is not an event by chance. It is a carefully planned act. We predicted that a huge revolt would happen in August 2023.

We are not saying that Russia is culling its soldiers, but the situation makes it look like that. Sanctions can make the situation tight.

So, Russia must reconsider its position regarding the level of difficulty in achieving its goals and retreat in line with the possible number of soldiers' deaths.

c} Russia if they genuinely believe that their retreating can pose an existential threat then they must cease attacking civilians and civilian infrastructure. After five hundred days of fighting such tactics cannot be tolerated as a way of bringing the other party to the negotiating table. Now such acts are becoming war crimes. Early days it could have been justified as a way of reducing the risks of the use of nuclear weapons. But after such a lengthy period one can argue that Russia now knows that Ukraine will not give in but will fight even for another 381 days. So, these tactics of attacking civilians become criminal acts, war crimes.

d} Russia must now seriously consider all avenues of peace. We can mediate peace talks. The Wagner revolt is a huge message for the Kremlin to reconsider the whole war. We believe that the real revolt will be in August of 2023. After such a long time without rotation of troops. This will make the war look like a death-grinding machine. Above all, Russia must consider if it can continue with the war until July 2024. There are so many options for peace.

i] A revert to prewar status.

This is still possible even though there are a large number of soldiers' deaths. It is not as bad as it will be 381 days from today. A prewar-status treaty can be agreed upon with Russia agreeing to pay for the destruction of the infrastructure. A return to a prewar situation and a return of all annexed regions. Or an agreement for these regions to be returned after some time has elapsed.

The other factor that supports this argument is the fact that Russia now knows that Ukraine can stand for itself and can square up to Russia on the battleground. NATO can refuse Ukraine's membership on the grounds that it is as equally strong as the alliance in terms of Russia. Russia, having known this, can now fear or act fast to deter the formation of a secret alliance between NATO and Ukraine. This is because the secret alliance will mean the secret handing out of nuclear weapons to Kyiv that can be used in Russia. So now Russia is in a position to negotiate as even a bigger existential threat is now posed by Ukraine and not NATO. This is very feasible in that NATO can still achieve the same goal of weakening Russia but without the blood on its hands. They can use Ukraine to do the dirty work through this secret alliance.

ii] The situation as it is but with some concessions.

Russia can make a treaty to return some of the annexed regions. Russia can argue that it has lost a lot of soldiers and can use this to justify holding to what they have. But there is a danger that forever Ukraine will feel bullied and abused, that forever they will look for avenues of revenge now or in the future. Ukraine might accept the rejection of its membership by NATO but form a secret alliance just to avenge the pain, suffering, and loss of its soldiers. All this is to make Russia pay one day. Especially considering that Ukraine considers itself as simply defending itself from the abuse by Russia. The secret alliance is to armor Ukraine with dangerous weapons. We believe that the admission by the West in supplying cluster bombs is a cover for even more dangerous weapons. We believe the secret alliance is to supply nuclear weapons to teach Russia a lesson. So, Russia must seriously consider making peace now.

iii] Continue with the status core and proceed in pressing Ukraine until there is regime change regardless of any secret alliance or their possession of nuclear weapons. The fact that Russia has a lot of nuclear weapons and their tactic of sending some nuclear weapons to Belarus means that they will not fear any secret alliance or whatever Ukraine does. They can seriously attack Kyiv aggressively. They might consider it better to have a full war with Ukraine now than entertain NATO later. We predicted that in July and August, Russia would fully join with Belarus and invade. But the Wagner group's revolt has highlighted another feasible option. We now believe that the Wagner will attack from Belarus or will be responsible for attacking Kyiv in September through missiles from the Belarus direction. This can mean that Russia can fully invade instead of retreating.

Nevertheless, we still recommend that Russia opt for peace. We can mediate the talks.

e} Russia must recognize Ukraine's sovereignty and any grievances can be negotiated through peace talks. We believe that a sovereign country cannot be invaded.

f} Russia must aim now to reduce the deaths of its soldiers. The presence of drones that can easily video the whereabouts of soldiers means high risks of these soldiers being ambushed and of their deaths. That means Russia will lose a lot of soldiers before they have made any impact. Remember your soldiers' lives are protected by our laws. No leader shall send soldiers to wars that are death-grinding machines.

Ukraine.

A country defending its sovereignty has to do whatever it takes to keep that sovereignty. This is one of our first principles. There are a lot of things that can strip off a country's sovereignty. Wars and invasions are the obvious factors but being in debt can have the same effect. Ukraine must also understand that it is not just Russia that can strip itself of its sovereignty. The West can have the same effect through 'foreign debt.'

1. A secret alliance with NATO.

Ukraine's resilience and courage have put them in equal standing to NATO on a one-to-one level. I would not be surprised if NATO refused its membership application to join the alliance. This is because Ukraine does not need to be a member of NATO to defend itself. They can defend themselves. What they might benefit from is a secret alliance with NATO where NATO provides weapons as needed and maintains the status quo. The advantage is that Russia might now come to the table because this is one of the reasons why they want regime change in Kyiv. If Ukraine cannot join NATO but still has a secret alliance treaty that offers the same benefits, Russia might withdraw its troops and make concessions.

The only danger from our point of view is that the secret alliance treaty will have no boundaries. This means that the West and NATO might provide nuclear weapons or dangerous bombs to Ukraine to use on Russia. This increases the risks of a nuclear war. Everyone is pointing at Russia as the one to use nuclear weapons, but Ukraine might be the one to use a nuclear weapon on Russia. Whatever the outcome Ukraine forever will fear bullying and abuse by Russia and the deaths of its soldiers and people will forever pain them and in the end, they will want to get even with Russia. Any future friction will see Ukraine use dangerous weapons, even a nuke. So remarkably high risks.

2. Settle for peace now.

We believe that this war will only increase the bargaining position of Ukraine but with the same result now. The only problem is that if this is to go on for another 381 days then obviously Ukraine will have lost more civilians, and soldiers and will have more infrastructure destroyed.

Will Ukraine's resilience, courage, and continued fight deter Russia in the future?

The question to ask is will Russia in the future back down or retreat just because it lost more soldiers fighting Ukraine? We do not think so. This resilience and courage are fitting when the enemy in Russia has no nuclear weapons. Secondly and is not fighting an existential threat. We have precedence in the USA-Japan war. Some might say that it was the Japanese resilience and stubbornness that brought about their destruction. If it were not for this surely the Americans would not have dropped those two bombs. We believe that Russia might fully invade Ukraine for they might consider it easier to invade Ukraine and effect regime change than to wait and fight NATO later.

Honestly, the world has realized that Ukraine might not even need to be a member of NATO. As I said, a secret alliance is all they need. If they can withstand five hundred days of Russian attack, they can go all the way to 881 days in total.

PART SEVEN

Strained relationship with the West and NATO.

The only risk to Ukraine is that NATO might now feel reluctant to help Ukraine in the future especially financially. The West around September might start to feel unappreciated by Ukraine; they will reduce their funding to a point where Kyiv cannot afford to pay their soldiers. Russia might threaten a Third World War that can put off the West and NATO in accepting Ukraine's membership choosing a secret alliance instead.

So, choosing peace now can be an excellent choice.

At the beginning of the war, Ukraine wanted to prove a point that they could fight the Russians on the battlefield and be able to win. Five hundred days into the war they have proved that, and they settled their bet. What else do they have to prove?

We as the new global leaders believe that anything undertaken from now will only increase the number of casualties with the same outcomes. So, it could be the best point in time to negotiate peace.

We strongly believe that even Ukrainians believed or wished that the war would end this July.

These are our reasons.

1. NATO membership has conditions, especially for former Soviet Union members. Prove your worthiness.

2. Prove you want NATO membership more and can fight and kill your former Soviet member to counteract the Trojan horse argument.

3. Prove you can be trusted and fit.

Surely after five hundred days, the Kyiv leadership was expecting NATO to announce a date for their membership. This would have meant a kick-out notice to the Russians to get out of Ukraine. This would have meant an end to the war. Or Russia would have fully invaded. This year is the July Kyiv leadership probably had in mind the war would end. But Russia, the West, and circumstances make it possible for the war to continue another 381 days.

The danger from continuing now is that the West and NATO feel like there is not much Ukraine can benefit from being a member. Ukraine's leadership can stand on its own. They can benefit from a secret alliance. NATO and the West were expecting a begging Ukraine. One that would run to them for help but instead, they got a fearless Ukraine who tells them what they think about them. This will now make them reduce support, especially financially.

The Kyiv regime might have difficulties even paying its soldiers as time goes on. Now if NATO wants the Ukraine regime to fail so that they feel like their protection is needed. Once Russia senses this it might literally set Kyiv on fire by September this year.

A possible revolt in Russia in August will have no impact and will be thwarted. So, continuing the war means tough times ahead. Yes, fighting can have an impact but only on the battleground with a trivial effect on the bargaining power at the end of the war.

Ukraine is now in limbo.

Any country fighting for its existence is justified in choosing what they think is right for them. There is no right or wrong. We only voice concerns because some decisions will mean more needless deaths of civilians which can be avoided.

Worse, some decisions can result in a nuclear war. An exceptionally good example similar in every way. Is the Japanese case. Even though it is not likely, at least for now. That Russia might use nuclear weapons on Ukraine. The risk will increase if another country or cult like NATO intervenes. This is what will increase the risks.

After vowing not to negotiate with the current Russian leadership Kyiv has technically put itself in limbo. Now is the time that was perfect for negotiating with Russia. Russia is fully aware now of its capabilities. This was the best time to negotiate. No one wants to go on for another 381 days. The Wagner revolt is proof of the frustration of the Russian soldiers with this war. Now everyone has felt the death-grinding machine that this war is. Now everyone wants peace, morals are low after such a long time. But after shutting all doors Ukraine is now in limbo. How to proceed from now? The only route left now is that dark road through the war's grinding machine. Another 381 days.

But do not panic, we are here as Tomorrow's World Order.

We can mediate fruitful negotiations. We aim to give everyone facts they can use to save lives. We are not here to encourage wars etc. but to stop wars. This is one way of doing that. Giving you all the facts so that you make informed decisions.

Our website www.twofuture.world

info@twofuture.world

0447719210295

NATO and the West.

A secret alliance with Ukraine might be all that is needed for peace's sake. This will revert everything to prewar status with the added advantage that they will from now act as if Ukraine is a member. Meaning coming to the rescue when needed and supplying the weapons and support for Ukraine to defend itself.

Or NATO can confirm the date of Ukraine's membership. This can deter Russia.

Continue with the funding and support of Ukraine.

The West has given Ukraine wings and must not withdraw that support. No matter what, this is what Ukraine wants. Fight Russia on its own on the battlefield and win. They can complain but NATO must understand that after such a long time of fighting stress, fatigue, and frustration can increase the tension.

NATO must not withdraw support now, especially financially.

Peace.

The West and NATO must push for peace. They can do this by reducing weapons supply but hinting at the date of Ukrainian membership to deter Russia from pushing on with the war.

Tomorrow's World Order

We are ready to mediate fruitful peace talks.

www.twofuture.world

info@twofuture.world

00447719210295

381 days to go.

This is a long time to go. After five hundred days of fighting this must feel like a lifetime. You all do not have to go with this war. You can easily decide to end this war today. We can mediate peace talks.

We have done our best to give all players involved our unbiased analysis of the circumstances. It is up to you all to make informed decisions and choose what is right not just for you but for all humanity.

You all can choose to continue fighting but we are here to make you aware of the consequences of each decision going forward.

Ignorance will not be a defense. Everyone is fully aware of the situation and the risks involved.

Any dangers you pose to civilians and even your soldiers can amount to breaches of international laws and our laws that protect everyone.

Make wise decisions today.

No one can win a nuclear war.

Sometimes it is an act of courage and being smart to opt for peace.

Ukraine has a right to defend itself.

Russia has no right to invade and attack a sovereign country.

But might have a right to protect itself against an existential threat.

You all have the power to refuse to go with this war-script and opt for peace today.

Only choosing peace means that everyone is a winner.

We have predicted how this war will end and we have empowered you all to fight this system and opt for peace. Value the lives of your people and the world might value you too.

On a global scale, we would not allow two countries to pose a risk of a nuclear war to the entire world. The failure to resolve your issues peacefully poses a real threat to all humanity. The world's weight is on your shoulders. Act wisely and opt for peace.

Five hundred days of fighting is enough. You proved your points. We now know you are all tough and can fight.

Now it is time to take things seriously and opt for peace.

Trust me, the world goes with your floor.

Choose war and some people will talk about this war. Those who have died through your war will have no say or right to contribute to this.

Choose peace and everyone will talk about peace and about you, and this is because you will have valued everyone's opinion. Meaning more people will talk about you.

No one is above the law; country, cult, or leader. If you ignore us one day justice will triumph.

Peace to all humankind.

Make the right decisions today.

We will put in a new system that will not depend on wars. But a system powered by technological advancements.

A New World Order where wars are the things of the past.

Welcome to Tomorrow's World Order.

Signed

17/July/2023

The First Global President of The World

David Gomadza

www.twofuture.world

info@twofuture.world

00447719210295

This book must be read in conjunction with all the books on the Russia and Ukraine war listed below.

See below.

A MUST READ!!

A Perfect Prediction: Russia-Ukraine War/Military Operation.

https://play.google.com/store/books/details/David_Gomadza_A_Pe
rfect_Predictio
n_Russia_Ukraine?id=PmaVEAAAQBAJ&hl=en_GB&gl=US

The First Global President of the World's Russia-Ukraine Peace Plan.: 07 March 2023.

https://play.google.com/store/books/details/David_Gomadza_The_First_Global_President_of_the_Wo?id=-aOyEAAAQBAJ&hl=en_GB&gl=US

Culling: The Sad Reality of The IMF and World Bank Loans as Triggers of Wars.: Finding Solutions to The Russian-Ukraine War.

https://play.google.com/store/books/details/David_Gomadza_Culling_The_Sad_Reality_of_The_IMF_a?id=mMluEAAAQBAJ&hl=en_GB&gl=US

Russia and Ukraine's Peace Treaty.: TOMORROW'S WORLD ORDER

https://play.google.com/store/books/details/David_Gomadza_Russia_and_Ukraine_s_Peace_Treaty?id=3Bd2EAAAQBAJ&hl=en_GB&gl=US

Tomorrow's World Order: A New Law & Order.: Dealing with Threats of Invasions, Wars and War Crimes.

https://play.google.com/store/books/details/David_Gomadza_Tomorrow_s_World_Order_A_New_Law_Ord?id=ws3ODwAAQBAJ&hl=en_GB&gl=US

An Order by The President of Tomorrow's World Order to Stop the War/Special Military Operation.: By Intervening, To Push Invaders Out of a Sovereign Nation.

https://play.google.com/store/books/details/David_Gomadza_An_Order_by_The_President_of_Tomorro?id=OtVtEAAAQBAJ&hl=

THE GREATSHIFT: 2023 IS THE YEAR OF THE GREATSHIFT TO SUSTAINABLE ENERGY [PHASE ONE-ELECTRIC VEHICLES].

ABOUT DAVID GOMADZA

I am the First Global President of the World.
We are here to introduce a new system that relies on technological advancement as the driver of the economy. Rather than weapons manufacturing as the current system that will in turn means forever wars.
We decoded the brain. Visit our website for proof.
www.twofuture.world

That means no one can lie to us.
We know everyone's thoughts.
We can time-travel even to the 1600s even to the time of the Egyptian pyramids' construction.
If you are serious about finding nothing-but-the-truth, then you come to the right people.
We are against the use of concealment tactics to age the entire world so that stress ages you all fast and kills you all.
The current system hides the things you need the answers to the most so that you worry too much and look for answers in the past thereby aging faster over time for the government to reduce its pension bill.
They rather have you dead early to save the pension money handouts.
But we think this is stupid as we can put things in place to make you earn even in your old age.
Information is power and you all have the right to know the truth.
We will stop going back in time to look for answers.
Everyone must look forward to the future. All answers we need are in the future.
Whatever happened in the past we have all the answers. Let us not look back for solutions otherwise, we will be stuck in this defensive stage in which we are in forever.
We must take you to another stage of development.
A stage where technology is the driver of the economy and not wars or weapons manufacturing as in this current stage.
There will not be wars ever again.

People shall not waste time looking back for answers to what happened in the past. This information will be freely available to all. We shall make people stress about the future only in a good way because the future arouses curiosity and imagination that keeps everyone young, energized, goal-driven, invigorated and rejuvenated and full of beans. Whereas the past fuels harmful stress to the body. The kind of stress that ages people faster. People shall find ways to earn income, things to write stories about, and talk about all in the future.

Let us look only to the future.

Are you ready?

I am.

Let us go.

Signed David Gomadza

The First Global

President of the World

www.twofuture.world

info@twofuture.world

00447719210295

VISIT OUR WEBSITE

www.twofuture.world